Learning to Create!

Teaching Real
DRAWING

By
Darcy Bell-Myers

**Cover and inside illustrations by
Darcy Bell-Myers**

Publishers
Instructional Fair · TS Denison
Grand Rapids, Michigan 49544

Dedication

To my husband, collaborator and friend, Bruce.
You always support, encourage and inspire me to be a "real" artist.
Thanks for all of those times you told me "It looks great!" and "Keep going!"

Credits
Author: Darcy Bell-Myers
Cover & Inside Illustrations: Darcy Bell-Myers
Project Director/Editor: Danielle de Gregory
Cover Art Director: Darcy Bell-Myers
Creative Director: Danielle de Gregory
Graphic Design: Darcy Bell-Myers
Graphic Layout: Deborah Hanson McNiff

About the Author
Darcy Bell-Myers has loved to draw since she was a little girl. Darcy has a B.F.A. from the Minneapolis College of Art & Design. She works as the art director for Instructional Fair · TS Denison in Minneapolis and lives with her husband, Bruce, and their two cats, Duncan and Pouncer.

INTRODUCTION

What can be more rewarding than watching the joy and excitement on a child's face as he or she learns to mix two colors together to form a new third color or beams proudly, showing you his or her first self-portrait? Learning to create is as natural as breathing, and children, if given the opportunity, encouragement and creative incentives, will blossom into competent, confident artists right before your very eyes!

Unfortunately, open-ended art activities are not always easy to find, and sometimes the idea of teaching children "real" art seems daunting. After all, isn't "real" art only for those select, elite "real artists"? Isn't "real" art difficult to understand, let alone create? To this I say, "Nonsense!" It just takes a little practice and some perseverance. All of the activities in this book are self-explanatory, and all offer step-by-step instructions, lists of materials and other resources to explore for more information if you feel the inclination to delve deeper into a particular subject.

All of us, at some point in our childhoods, were creative. Some of us were nurtured and supported in our creativity, but sadly, some of us learned to be afraid of creativity, or even that there was only one "correct" way to be creative—that our own personal ways were wrong. You have the opportunity to nurture the creativity in a youngster, to add something to that child's life and perhaps, to even open that door a bit wider for yourself.

Good luck in your creative adventure and have fun!

TABLE OF CONTENTS

CARTOONING

CREATIVE IMAGINATIVE

TWO MINUTE INTENSIVES

A Few Words about Materials

The world of art materials can be a confusing, daunting and expensive one. Because of this, I have tried to recommend commonly found media. Most of the materials needed for this book are basic ones that can be found in your local art supply store. Where more inexpensive solutions are available, I have tried to recommend them. Luckily, supplies for drawing, as opposed to those for painting, sculpture, multimedia, or many other artistic pursuits, are relatively inexpensive or at least long-lasting. Pencils, charcoal, conté crayon, and other basic drawing media are very affordable. Even though a good set of pastels might be expensive, if properly cared for, it will last for years.

To create a drawing requires only pencil, paper and eraser. However, I suggest that you and your young artists experiment with different types of art pencils, papers and erasers as well as with other media. Sometimes a chalky pastel can lend a certain atmosphere to a work of art that would be unattainable with a regular pencil. Also, the standard number two pencil that is common in schools does not have the rich black color of a soft art pencil, nor does it come in the variety of shapes and sizes that art pencils do. This small investment is well worth the effort. When it comes to purchasing paper (probably the most expensive material needed for drawing), use common sense. If the class is doing quick gesture drawings, use cheap newsprint. However, if students will be laboring over a detailed portrait, a good quality paper that does not tear with repeated erasing or a paper in a striking color could aid and inspire your class.

Here are a few kinds of art materials you may want to try for activities in this book:

bamboo brushes: Bamboo brushes were originally intended for use in Japanese calligraphy but are relatively inexpensive and can be used with a variety of waterbased paints .

chalk: Chalk is the same thing as pastel—but pastels are of a higher quality. Still, regular colored chalks can be a good and inexpensive alternative to pastels. Use "sidewalk" chalks to turn your playground blacktop into a colorful and non-permanent artistic masterpiece.

charcoal: Charcoal has been used to draw since the first artists pulled it out of fires and made pictures on cave walls thousands of years ago. It may be purchased in sticks that can be smudged and blended in a messy but fun way or in pencils which tend to be neater. I know of artists who make their own charcoal—a fun and interesting project.

clips: Use jumbo clips to attach students' works to their drawing boards when going outside or when using drawing boards in the classroom.

conté crayon: This is a material much like pastel or charcoal, but easier to control. Conté crayons come in sticks or pencils and in a variety of earthy colors from russet red to deep black.

drawing board: Drawing boards are one of those things that at first seem like an extra but quickly become essential. They can be purchased or home-made (usually made of masonite with a cutout at the top to use as a handle). With papers clipped or taped to drawing boards, students may go outside to draw. Inside, they can be propped against a tabletop for a better angle when drawing.

india ink: This is a black, permanent ink that can be used either with pens or brushes to create striking effects. Thin it with water to achieve grays.

ink pens: Ink pens in a variety of shapes and sizes are a great drawing tool. Try dipping pens with nibs, such as "crow quill" or markers in a variety of shapes and sizes from fine point to thick. Calligraphy markers are also great to use.

kneaded eraser: Use a gum or kneaded eraser to erase more dusty drawing materials such as pastel, charcoal or conté crayon. It erases cleanly and can be kneaded like dough to expose a clean surface. Your students will love to play with these!

paper: There are many different kinds of paper that come in a variety of price ranges. Use newsprint for practice exercises and plain white or colored sheets for other projects. Plentiful amounts of paper in large size sheets will inspire your class to work with enthusiasm and not fear "wasting" paper. For charcoal, pastel and conté, a paper with some kind of texture or "tooth" is good.

pastels, chalk: Soft, delicate, chalky pastels are messier than oil pastels, but can be used to beautiful effect. They are easily blended and fun to use on colored paper. Good pastels can be surprisingly expensive, but are essential for any artist serious about drawing.

pastels, oil: These are the most commonly found pastels in schools because they are not as messy or expensive as the chalk type. Try Cray-pas for a less expensive alternative. For a unique and painterly effect, try using them with a brush dipped in odorless mineral spirits, paint thinner or liquin.

pencil: There are many different kinds of pencils in different hardnessess, shapes and points. If a light, sketchy effect is desired, use a harder pencil labeled with a number and an "H." If a darker, smudgier look is desired, use a softer "B" pencil. For most of the projects in this book, I suggest the softer "B" pencils or soft brands like Ebony. Some interesting and different kinds of pencils to try are woodless ones (composed entirely of graphite) and chisel-shaped "carpenter's" pencils, which must be sharpened with a knife.

sketchbook: A sketchbook is essential for a young artist to practice drawing, to have on hand when inspiration strikes, and even to write down ideas for future projects. It may be a simple unlined notebook, a beautiful hardbound journal or anything in-between.

tortillons or blending stumps: These are inexpensive little paper cones which could be used to blend pastels, charcoal and conté crayons. They save wear and tear on fingers, which could be rubbed raw after hours of blending.

watercolor pencils or crayons: These can be used just like regular colored pencils or crayons, but when a wet brush is added, they turn into paint. They can also be dipped in water and used for drawing to create many beautiful effects. They produce a painterly effect but are more controllable. Use brands such as Caran D'Ache for face painting.

SETTING UP A DRAWING BOARD

The use of a simple masonite drawing board allows artists to draw anywhere, anytime! Another good reason to use a drawing board is that it can be propped against a table edge—angling the work to a more comfortable position. Use tape or jumbo clips to hold paper in place and you are ready to go!

PORTRAITURE

IMPRESSIONISTIC PASTEL PORTRAITS

In this exercise, the students get a chance to create their own impressionist pastel portraits. This is a good introduction to portraiture and, if your students enjoy this project, you may later choose to move on to painted portraits.

A good way to start is by showing students examples of many different kinds of impressionist art, especially pastel pictures of people, since that is what your young artists will be creating. Many of the impressionists such as Edgar Degas, Berthe Morisot or Mary Cassatt did lovely pastel pictures which will inspire your class. You may talk to your class about how these artists drew and painted people close to them, such as family, friends, people in neighborhood cafés, or local performers. In this exercise, your class draws people familiar to them.

STUDIO

Ask everyone in class to choose a partner. Students take turns first posing, then drawing their partners. Since the impressionists showed people involved in everyday activities, the portraits may show an everyday activity as well, or the model simply sitting still. Remind your class to look closely as they draw and to try to fill in all the white space with vibrant, impressionistic color. When finished, spray your masterpieces in a well-ventilated area with fixative or hair spray to keep them from smudging.

Materials
- chalk
- colored pastels
- pastel paper or paper with some "tooth"
- kneaded erasers

Optional
- tortillons

WHODUNIT?

In this exercise, students get to practice being real-life police artists. They have to use their powers of observation and language skills to describe the appearance of someone seen only briefly or their imaginations to portray in portrait form a person that is unknown to them.

Police artists help to solve crimes by being able to draw portraits of people that they have never even seen! How do they do this? By asking detailed questions of a witness who *has* seen the subject that they are trying to draw. In this exercise your class will get an opportunity to try being "detective artists."

STUDIO

Divide the class in half. One half of the class at a time gets to be "detectives," and the other half the "witnesses." It is important to separate the two groups so that only the witnesses see the face of the "suspect" to be drawn. Bring in your suspect (a parent or school volunteer) for the witness group to study. If a volunteer is not available, you may show a photograph of some random person, although it is more exciting to have a real volunteer come to class! Depending on how elaborate you wish to make this exercise, you may have your volunteer commit a "crime" (such as stealing a chair) or just stand for a few minutes in front of the class. This is a good time to discuss how difficult it is to remember details about something that is seen only briefly. This is why it can be hard for police to find witnesses, or why witnesses often have disparate descriptions of a suspect.

Pair the students so that each detective artist has a witness to question. By these questions alone (with no names of suspects given), the artist must draw the suspect as accurately as possible. Questions that might be helpful could be: "Was the suspect male or female?" "Approximately what age was the suspect?" "What clothes was he or she wearing?" "Did the suspect remind you of anyone famous?" "What shape was her or his face—round, oval or square?" "What length and color hair did he or she have?" "Were there any distinguishing characteristics, such as moles, freckles, dimples, beard, or moustache?"

Materials
- **soft pencils**
- **erasers**
- **large sheets of white paper**
- **volunteer "criminal" or a photograph**

When your drawings are complete, bring the volunteer back into the classroom to see how your detective artists did. How close did they get? Ask them which drawings are the most accurate and why? If there is time, switch roles so that all the class has a chance to be a detective. (Of course, you will need a second "criminal.")

PERSONALITY PORTRAITS

Some of the most beautiful portraits drawn by artists are of the artists' friends and families going about the everyday business of their lives. In this exercise, students have an opportunity to create portraits that show more of the subjects and, therefore, more *about* the subjects, revealing deeper insights into the characters of the people being drawn.

Begin by showing students the drawings of Jean Auguste Dominique Ingres. In addition to being a brilliant painter, Ingres created many beautiful pencil drawings. His portraits in particular show a deep insight into the personalities of the people he portrayed. One such portrait, *Portrait of Charles Gounod*, shows a young man, a friend of the artist, seated at the piano. Although this portrait was created long ago in 1841, this young man seems as familiar as someone we would know today.

STUDIO

For this project, students try to create portraits that show the majority of the poser's body—from the knees up—and also to give insight into the personality and interests of this person.

Choose a volunteer from the class to model for you. Have the class think long and hard about how best to represent this person. Is this someone who likes to play a sport? Then show her or him engaged in that sport.

Is this someone who plays an instrument or acts in school plays? Then get the person to pose as if doing one of these things. Also, ask your artists to think about the personality of their model. Is this a shy, quiet person or the class clown? Have them not just render the person's physical appearance, but try to tell the viewer more about his or her personality through the drawing.

Materials
- pencils
- erasers
- paper
- model engaged in something he or she likes to do

SENSATIONAL SELF-PORTRAITS

Self-portraits are a fun, exciting and relatively easy form of portrait to create. Why easy? Because you can always get yourself to pose and to sit still for as long as needed. It is fascinating to explore your own uniqueness through art!

Explain to students that self-portraits are an important tradition in art. Show students some examples of self-portraits. Choose either drawings or paintings by artists, such as Vincent van Gogh, Albrecht Dürer or Rembrandt. What do the swirling backgrounds of van Gogh's self-portraits tell us about his turbulent personality? What does the careful, studied, draftsman-like quality of Dürer's self-portraits tell us about his? What do the settings of these self-portraits tell us?

It is also interesting to see how artists' self-portraits change over time. There are many changes between the early self-portraits of Rembrandt painted when he was a young man and the self-portraits created when he was older; yet, we can still see that they are painted by the same person. Your class may be surprised to know that an artist could paint a self-portrait every day of the week and that each painting would be different from the next because people's feelings and perceptions change constantly.

STUDIO

Give each student paper and his or her own mirror, if possible. (Students can bring mirrors from home.) Each student needs to decide on a composition, lighting and setting for a self-portrait that reflects her or his own personality. Remind your class to keep looking at their mirrors—this will enable them to achieve good likenesses. Ask students to begin by drawing the basic shapes of their portraits lightly in pencil before using the conté crayon. As they work, encourage them to work on the entire picture at once, rather than finishing only one small portion at a time, such as the eyes. This will help your artists to keep the proportions accurate. When done, ask the students if they can tell which drawing was done by whom? What enables them to tell? Which features portray the personalities of the artists most accurately?

Materials
- pencils
- conté crayons
- kneaded erasers
- paper with some "tooth" or texture
- mirrors (preferably self-standing ones such as makeup mirrors)

REFLECTIONS ON ART

In this exercise, each student is given one-half of the image of a face from a magazine, museum postcard, catalog, or other source. The student tries to duplicate the other half of the face as closely as possible, mirror-image style. This is good practice for learning to see human proportions accurately and improving attention to detail.

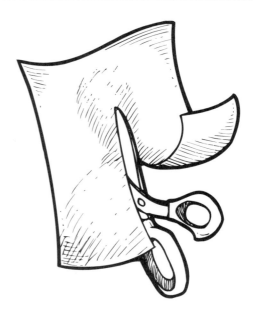

STUDIO

Many famous artists copied work that they admired or worked from photographs in order to learn how to draw and paint better. Even famous artists were once students, just like your class, and had to work hard. This is a good thing to remind your class when they get discouraged. Every artist has trouble rendering certain subjects. Looking at how other artists tackled similar problems or looking at photographs can be quite helpful. Look at books about the lives of artists which show their student work. Some books even show the photographs that artists, such as Maxfield Parrish or Grandma Moses, routinely used.

Let your students choose images that they wish to mirror, then cut the images in half, vertically down the center of the face. (Use a ruler in order to get a straight line.) Next, have each student glue only one half of the image to her or his paper. Be sure that when gluing they leave enough room to paint the other halves of the pictures. Finally, ask each student to draw the missing half of the face. Remind your young artists to look very closely as they copy—matching proportions, values (lights and darks) and details as exactly as possible!

Materials
- **magazines or museum postcards with frontal closeups of faces**
- **erasers**
- **heavy paper**
- **dark soft pencils**
- **scissors**
- **glue**
- **rulers**

TAKING SIDES

Silhouettes are challenging but intriguing to draw. It is more common to draw portraits showing three-quarters of a person's face or a view that is frontal, even though silhouettes can show great depth of character and be visually quite dynamic. For this project, students create silhouette portraits of classmates, and they learn to view portraiture from a different angle—literally!

Look at silhouette drawings with students. Henri de Toulouse-Lautrec created some striking silhouettes in his *At the Moulin Rouge* and *Aristide Bruant* posters. Paula Modersohn-Becker's *Portrait of a Peasant Woman* shows a silhouette of a peasant woman depicted in a way that shows the cares the woman has had in her life. Yet, through the means of the profile view, the artist is able to show the strength and nobility of her subject's spirit in her uplifted chin.

STUDIO

Divide the class into groups of two with one person drawing the other and then switching so that everyone has an opportunity to draw. Students must draw in the profile view. Remind students to measure visually the distances among features. Generally, the eyes are halfway down the head but students often tend to place them too high and too near the front of the profile.

Materials
- pencils
- erasers
- conté crayons or charcoals
- lightly textured paper

SUPER STAR SKETCHES

Artists have long created images of famous people—kings and queens, writers, actors, poets, and politicians. For this project, students are "commissioned" to create portraits of famous people in pastels.

Show students portraits of famous people throughout the ages. These could include the portraits of royalty drawn by Francisco de Goya, portraits of nobility by Rosalba Carriera or portraits of stage personalities drawn by Henri de Toulouse-Lautrec.

Before photography was invented, portraits were not just the only means of recording what a person looked like; they were also a means of glorifying a person's importance and influence. Portraits were commissioned to record different kinds of special events, to generate large donations for the church, and even, in the case of one portrait commissioned to Rosalba Carriera, to display the sitter's beauty in order to help her find a suitable husband!

STUDIO

For this exercise, your students pretend that they have been commissioned to create a portrait of a celebrity, political figure or other famous person of their choice. Using photographs as a guide, they must try to create portraits that represent this movie star, musician, president, etc., so well that others in the class can tell whom the portrait is supposed to represent. Ask students to use pastels after first sketching their portraits in pencil. Remind them to refer to the photographs often.

Students should not be limited to drawing just what is in the photograph. Encourage them to choose settings and props that add to the subject. When done, spray the portraits with fixative or hair spray and ask the class to try to guess whom each of the drawings represents.

Materials
- **pencils**
- **erasers**
- **chalk pastels**
- **pastel (lightly textured) paper**
- **photographs of famous people**

FIGURE DRAWING

INVEST IN YOUR GESTURE

The idea behind the kind of practice drawing known as "gesture" drawing is to capture an object or person quickly and spontaneously. Many famous artists have done gesture drawings, and you can let your class know that this is a little-known technique artists use to get the initial "feel" of something that they are trying to draw.

Students make many drawings for this exercise during the course of the class. A student throws aside one sheet of paper and starts fresh on the next, spending only minutes on each drawing. The goal in this exercise is spontaneity—a natural and uninhibited way of drawing. The constant insistence on realistic depictions can create a critical or negative attitude toward drawing—not very much fun. Surprisingly, drawings done spontaneously often have a natural, unconscious realism that does not occur in more labored drawings.

STUDIO

Ask for a student volunteer to strike a pose in front of the class. Give the students a pre-set amount of time to capture the pose before asking your student model to move to another pose. Start off with about five minutes or more and move progressively to two-minute, one-minute and even thirty-second poses. Be sure to let children take turns being the "model." If a student is unsure what kind of pose to strike, suggest that he or she pretend to be doing something ordinary (reading a book, playing baseball). Also, be sure to have students write their names and the amount of time spent on each drawing before putting it aside.

Ask your young artists to try to capture the feeling of what they see. Instead of painstakingly working on drawing a single part of the model, ask them to quickly scribble the entire form of the model. Ask your students to follow the flow of the drawings in sweeping strokes, taking their pencils off their papers as little as possible. Although at first your young students may be frustrated with such a small amount of time to draw, you will find that they quickly become excited with this fast-paced adventurous drawing. Before your class time is up, be sure to ask them which their favorite drawings are and why. Can they tell what the people in each others' drawings are doing? Whom do the drawings depict? Do they like better the drawings that took longer to make?

Materials
- **soft pencils, charcoal or conté crayons**
- **kneaded erasers**
- **many large sheets of inexpensive drawing paper (such as newsprint)**
- **egg timer or wristwatch**

HANDSOME HANDS

Hands are one of the hardest parts of the body to draw, yet it is easy for students to practice by drawing their own hands in different positions and from different angles. In this exercise, students do just that. By studying hands closely, your artists gain more confidence as they portray hands realistically and expressively. This helps young artists become more comfortable drawing hands in their other figure drawings.

STUDIO

Show students as many examples of drawings of hands as possible, Albrecht Dürer's *Praying Hands*, for example, or any portrait in which the hands are included. The hand is one feature that can be confusing to draw in proportion to itself and to the rest of the body. It may be helpful to remember that the outstretched hand is roughly the same size as the face. It may also be helpful for students to trace their hands on paper to better see the relationship and proportions of the fingers to the palm.

Pass out materials and have students pose the hand with which they do not draw and carefully trace its contours in the air with the tips of their pencils. Then, ask them to draw the contours on the paper, looking continuously back at their hands and tracing the edges cleanly. When done, ask them to change to new poses and to keep drawing in order that each student completes an entire page of studies. As artists, they should think not just about each individual drawing, but about how the drawings relate on the page to form a composition. The composition as a whole should be as pleasing as each individual study.

Materials
- **soft pencils**
- **erasers**
- **paper**

TOPSY TURVY TREATMENTS

Sometimes it helps to look at something in a fresh way in order to be able to draw it better. Many artists routinely look at a work in progress in the mirror to better see its flaws. For this project, your artists look upside down for inspiration.

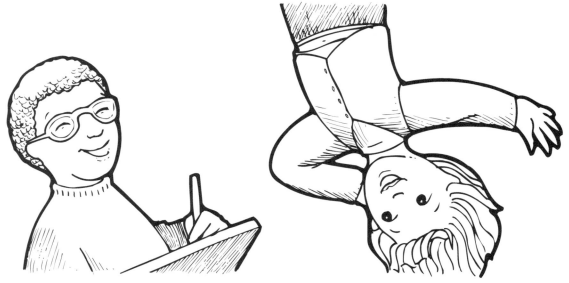

STUDIO

Before class, hang a photographic portrait poster upside down, and cover it with blank paper. When your students are present, hand out paper and supplies. Pull away the paper to reveal the poster upside down, and ask students to copy it. This may seem strange at first, after all, is it not harder to draw something upside down? Ironically, it is not. Our eyes get used to seeing things in one set way. We prepare to draw an eye and we draw it in a set "formula" because we have always "seen" an eye in this way. The idea behind this exercise is for students to draw the shapes and values that make up an eye, not a preset formula.

Students may be frustrated at first and try to turn things back around, but calmly insist they draw the image upside-down, as if it were an abstract design.

You and your artists will be surprised at the realistic results they achieve. Remind them that the next time they draw something right side up, they might remember the lessons learned from this exercise.

Materials
- pencils
- erasers
- photographic portrait poster
- paper

SPORTS SHORTS

Young artists need all the practice they can get when it comes to drawing people, especially in different positions and showing different movements. Drawings of athletes are great practice for this as well as an interesting subject matter for students.

Look at some examples of art created by artists interested in portraying athletics or dance, such as Henri Toulouse-Lautrec's pictures of jockeys or Edgar Degas's drawings of ballet dancers.

STUDIO

Ask students to chose one kind of sport or dance that they would like to draw, and ask them to create a series of drawings (three is a good number) on that theme. They might choose to watch the school soccer team practice and draw the players, draw baseball players from television or take their sketchbooks to ballet class—whatever interests and inspires them will bring the best results. Have your students show the rest of the class their favorite drawings and discuss why they like them.

Materials
- pencils
- erasers
- sketchbooks or paper clipped to drawing boards

MINUTE MARVELS

In this exercise, students do a series of small, timed drawings and try to see how much can be represented in a short amount of time.

Begin by showing students full-length portrait drawings by famous artists; light, quick sketches as opposed to more studied pictures. Look at the simple line drawings of Henri Matisse or sketches by Mary Cassatt. What these drawings have in common is that they are quick studies done in a series. The drawings flowed from the artist's pencil, and then the artist moved on to something else.

STUDIO

Have students divide into pairs, taking turns drawing and being drawn. As these are quick renderings, each student should pose for no more than ten minutes. Ask students to create as finished a drawing as possible in that time frame, showing the personality of the model as well as his or her position. Use inexpensive paper for this exercise because students will complete many drawings in the course of the class. Inexpensive paper not only saves you money, it also encourages students to create many drawings and allows them to start over if drawings do not develop the way they wish.

When students are finished with a series of drawings (four or five), ask them to choose their favorites. Put the drawings up on the wall if you like, and discuss what is most successful about each of them and why.

Materials
- pencils
- erasers
- newsprint or other inexpensive paper
- egg timer

Poster Pizazz

In this exercise, students look at the work of famous impressionist artist Toulouse-Lautrec and create their own poster art just like Toulouse-Lautrec did!

The work of Henri de Toulouse-Lautrec is admired for its graphic contrasts, bright colors and interesting characterizations of local performers. His posters, created from famous Parisian sights, such as the Moulin Rouge, are classics that can inspire your class. Toulouse-Lautrec was a sad figure, having broken both of his legs in his teens, he was crippled and an outcast. He turned to the nightlife of Paris and created striking posters of local performers for cabaret shows.

STUDIO

Your class is probably not familiar with cabarets, but movies make a good comparison. Ask your class to create a movie poster featuring a star performer or scene in the style of Toulouse-Lautrec—bold outlines and bright graphic shapes. Your artists' posters will not be printed with lithography—the method Toulouse-Lautrec used—but this look can be simulated with oil pastel outlines filled in with watercolor or tempera washes. The oil pastel "resists" the water-based paint and creates a dramatic look. The title of the movie can be of the students' creation or choosing, but it should be boldly and creatively drawn.

Materials
- pencils
- erasers
- oil pastels
- tempera or watercolor paints

MATISSE MASTERPIECE

Henri Matisse was a master at creating lyrical and rich figure drawings with a few simple lines. For this exercise, students create simple and graceful line drawings in the style of Matisse.

Matisse could create amazingly detailed drawings with a minimum of lines. His paper cutouts also reflect this beautiful simplicity, but for this exercise, show students some of his drawings. Note the delicate floral prints and the suggestion of textured fringe in some of his works. Discuss with students the fact that his compositions fill the entire page, yet still feel uncluttered.

STUDIO

Set up a still life of your own, starting with a patterned cloth draped against a table with books on it (or anything else easily available), and ask for a student volunteer to sit in a chair in front of this set-up. Remind students to let their pencils flow freely and try not to erase—simply move on to another drawing. When students have finished their first drawings, have a different student be the next model.

Materials
- dark, soft pencils such as Ebony pencils
- erasers
- smooth white paper. such as bond paper
- textured and patterned cloth, remnants or throws
- still-life materials

STILL LIFE

EMOTIONAL OBJECTS

This exercise helps students to add feeling to their work. They take ordinary, common objects and portray them in unusual and emotional ways.

STUDIO

Begin by asking students to bring an object to class to draw. This object can be any common object at all, from a hat to a bar of soap. Have each student write a few descriptive words (especially words describing feelings) on scraps of paper, such as mad, sad, joyful, tense, jealous, etc.

Place all of the scraps in a hat and have the students each pull out a few. Using these adjectives, the students make series of small drawings of their objects. For example, if the artist's object is a hat and he or she selects the word "mad," then the drawing will be of a "mad hat." This exercise helps create some unusual pieces of art and teaches students to see objects in new ways. Artists are often called upon to portray a person, place or thing in an emotional way. In this way, a picture of a house could be "nostalgic"; a portrait of someone admired could show that person to be "regal"; or an ordinary object, such as a cane leaning in a corner, could be "sad."

Materials
- **pencils**
- **watercolor pencils or crayons**
- **brushes**
- **paper**
- **objects brought from home**

TOTALLY WIRED

In this exercise, students get inspiration from the work of Alexander Calder—an artist who created wire-frame mobiles and drawings that had the look of wire. Students create their own wire images and learn about seeing shapes more three-dimensionally.

Show students the work of Calder, and show how his drawings look like they are crafted of wire. In some, it looks as though wire bends around the edges, making the drawing appear very three-dimensional.

STUDIO

Ask your young artists to imagine that the objects in the still life have wire wrapped around them and to draw the shape that that wire would form. They must think about all three dimensions of the objects and draw with their pencils the form that the wire would take. This can be tricky, but it is good practice.

As an additional exercise, you might let them create their own wire sculptures and mobiles like Calder's and then make drawings of them.

Materials
- ink fine-line pens
- paper
- still-life objects

In this exercise, students learn to portray light and shadow in drawings. By drawing with both white and black chalk on gray paper, students focus on how light and shadow play across the different surfaces of the still life. By dramatically emphasizing lights and darks, this activity helps students to create more three-dimensional images.

For a nice introduction to the topic of light and shadow, show students the paintings and drawings of Rembrandt. Rembrandt was a master at creating mood, atmosphere and dimension in his images through the interplay of light and shadow. Ask students why they think Rembrandt chose to leave so much of the area of his compositions shrouded in shadow. Does this create a certain feeling to his work?

STUDIO

Spread the dark cloth on a tabletop, and then set up the still life of found objects. The objects can be any that are easily accessible. It is helpful to choose objects of different textures and shapes, particularly things like shiny glass bottles or metallic cans that have interesting highlights and reflections to draw. Include a round baseball or a square box—items with basic shapes that students can practice with ease. Aim the spotlight at the still life, being sure to direct the light so that shadows are cast for the artists to draw. Accurately drawing the cast shadows can add solidity and dimensionality to an otherwise flat-looking drawing. If it is possible, dim the lights in the rest of the room to accentuate the effect of this contrast.

When the students are ready to begin drawing, ask them to rough out the shapes lightly in pencil and then proceed drawing the lightest areas they see with the white chalk or pastel—the white highlight of the rim of a vase, for example. They can use their fingers or a blending tool to smudge the chalks and achieve a variety of grays. It is important that they look carefully at the still life and refer to it continuously as they draw. Remind them to draw the shadows that fall across the tabletop. When your class's drawings are finished, spray them with fixative or hair spray in a well-ventilated area.

Materials
- pencils
- gray pastel paper
- white and black chalk, pastels or pastel pencils
- kneaded erasers
- still-life objects
- black cloth
- clamp spotlight
- fixative or hair spray

ENCHANTING PLANTS

Students learn that carefully drawing an object helps us to better understand it. This project presents just such an opportunity!

Show students the work of artists, such as Maria Sibylla Merian or John James Audubon, who used their artwork to understand better and to document the natural world. Your young artists can follow in the footsteps of these great naturalists and create their own botanical or zoological drawings.

STUDIO

If it is possible, take the class outside to draw or collect plants and flowers. Otherwise, you may let them either bring plants from home or use library books (such as the National Audubon Society publications) as references.

Have students sketch in pencil first, adding ink and watercolor last. Try to have waterproof ink in the black pens, or add ink last when the watercolor is dry to avoid the ink bleeding into the paint. Label your lovely creations with their scientific names and lean back admiringly!

Materials
- **pencils**
- **black ink pens**
- **watercolor paints or watercolor pencils**
- **paper**
- **plants, flowers or animals**

ACCENTUATE THE NEGATIVE

In this project, students learn the concept of "negative space"—any space in a composition that is not the subject. Part of what renders a composition compelling is when both the positive and negative shapes are interesting. Through this exercise, students begin to see their compositions as wholes that include not only the subject matter but the non-subject matter as well.

Look at a variety of still-life drawings with students. What is the negative space in these images? Is it not more interesting to see various shapes in a composition rather than a single object placed in the center?

STUDIO

Arrange the still-life objects on a table and ask students to begin by lightly sketching them. (However, the students must concentrate on drawing the space around the object rather than the object itself.) Ask students to use the markers to fill in the negative and positive spaces in contrasting colors and textures.

Materials
- pencils
- magic markers
- paper
- variously shaped objects for still life arrangement

ON A SHOESTRING

For this project, students create "contour," or line drawings, of common objects—their shoes!

Contour drawings, or line drawings, that follow the edges or contours of something, are fun to draw and good practice. Look at some examples of contour drawings such as those by Matisse.

STUDIO

Ask students to take off one shoe each and put it on the table at an interesting angle. They should carefully look at where the edges begin and end, and follow those edges around the shoe first with their pencils, tracing the contours in the air. Then they can draw the contours on their papers. Their eyes should be on the shoes as much as possible.

Materials
- pencils
- erasers
- students' shoes
- large sheets of paper

A good practice exercise is to have students draw the shoes, trying not to look at their papers at all!

THE MAGIC OF FABRIC

Being able to create drawings of fabric, or "drapery studies," is an important yet tricky skill that was often taught in the traditional art academies of Europe. By allowing students to focus on drawing how fabric moves and drapes, this exercise helps them to create more realistic drawings of people dressed in capes, gowns or just ordinary clothing. It is often helpful for students to focus and work on certain aspects that challenge them. This exercise does just that.

Look at images where artists have drawn fabrics—the sculptural drapes of Michelangelo, the funny *Six Pillows* drawn by Albrecht Dürer or gauzy folds by Parmigianino.

STUDIO

Set up your own still life of fabrics draped across chairs or hanging from table edges. Have a strong light source. Ask students to draw studies of the folds using the charcoal or conté crayons to carefully represent the lights and darks. Have each of the students create a page of several studies arranged artistically. Remember, it is not enough to draw realistically; the composition should be thought-out and work as a piece of art in its own right.

It is fun for your artists to apply this knowledge to other drawings, perhaps a wizard with a billowing cape or a princess in a long, flowing dress.

Materials
- **pencils**
- **charcoal or conté crayons in black and white**
- **kneaded erasers**
- **pale colored paper**
- **fabric to drape (old sheets)**

LANDSCAPE & ANIMALS

In this exercise, students learn about a style of Japanese art exemplified by simple, clean strokes, and bold, uncluttered compositions. They try creating their own *sumi-e*, or Japanese brush and ink paintings.

Begin by showing your young artists examples of any Japanese brush and ink paintings that you can find. If possible, find pictures of ink paintings of the fifteenth-century Japanese master Sesshu and the prints of nineteenth-century artists Katsushika Hokusai and Ando Hiroshige. The latter two are artists whose ink drawings were carved into wood blocks and then printed. These artists are admired for the simplicity, boldness and poetry of their works. Like the Japanese form of poetry *haiku*, these ink drawings seek to make a rich and powerful statement with as few elements as possible. The idea behind this style of art is to say the most with the least, to think carefully before making a brush stroke, and to make each brush stroke be as descriptive as it can be.

STUDIO

Ask students to begin by getting their inspiration from Japanese artists such as those mentioned above. Have them copy some of the brush strokes; practice using the ink to create washes, lines and textures, and then begin compositions of their own. They should create their own ink paintings in the *sumi-e* style, using real leaves and flowers as models, if available. If this is not possible, students may look at photographs. It is helpful to have some Japanese artists' work around for inspiration and guidance in this gentle and graceful tradition.

It should be noted that, of all the materials used in this book, india ink has the most potential for mess. It does not come out of clothing, once dried. For this reason, I suggest a few precautions: Tape drop cloths or paper to desks or tables; tape down ink bottles to the tables, and have your young sumi-e artists wear smocks.

Materials
- bamboo or watercolor brushes
- black india ink
- palettes or plates
- jars of clean water
- heavyweight paper
- scrap paper
- books of Japanese art
- smocks

Optional
- flowers and leaves

TERRIFIC TEXTURED TERRAINS

In this exercise, students have an opportunity to create multi-textured landscape pictures, using the work of Vincent van Gogh as inspiration.

Van Gogh created beautiful and turbulent drawings, similar in mood and texture to his paintings, but done completely in black and white with ink pen on paper. Show your students some examples of these drawings. You might wish to show them one drawing in particular, entitled simply *Cypresses*. Interestingly, this drawing is almost exactly the same in composition and texture to his famous *Starry Night* painting. It would be helpful to show both works to students, so they can see how an image changes when translated between different mediums.

STUDIO

When your students are ready to create their own textured pictures, have them take drawing boards outside, if possible, to see the real textures of leaves, stone, bark, etc. This will help them create different and more realistic kinds of textures for their projects. Otherwise, have your artists refer to photographs. Ask them to use pens, brushes or any other means to create textures, as many different different kinds of textures as possible—dots, slashes or feathery swirls. Lines can be spaced closely together or far apart and be fat or thin.

Materials
- pencils
- black ink pens with different sizes of nibs or tips
- paper
- drawing boards (for outdoors) or landscape photographs

PET PORTRAITS

Pets are special members of our families. In this project, students get to create a lasting momento in the form of a portrait of that four-footed furry or that finned and fishy friend.

STUDIO

Ask students to bring in photographs of their pets. If this is not possible, try to have some library books with pictures of various animals or pets available. If a student does not have a pet, she or he may draw the kind of pet the student would wish to have.

Ask students to begin by sketching and then proceed to adding the watercolor pencil. Remind students to be aware of the texture of fur, scales or whiskers and to try to capture that texture with different line weights. One great thing about using the watercolor pencil is that this medium can either be left to look like normal colored pencil, or with the addition of a wet brush, turned into paint. Ask students to choose carefully which parts of their pictures have the gentle, even look of the wash and which have the cross-hatching and texture of pencil. Experiment with layering these techniques.

Materials
- pencils
- erasers
- watercolor pencils
- brushes
- watercolor paper
- photographs of pets or other animals
- jars of clear water

CLOSE UP, FAR AWAY

Perspective is an interesting concept—it basically means that things appear to get smaller the further they are from the viewer.

Talk about the concept of perspective with students. Why is it that railroad tracks or roads seem to get narrower as they move away from us? Why is it that things from the view of an airplane window seem tiny? The answer is perspective. The conscious use of perspective in Western art was not common until the Renaissance, which is why many medieval drawings seem so flat. Show students comparisons between Medieval art and Renaissance art for a better grasp of this idea.

STUDIO

For a real-life demonstration of this concept, take students to a glass door or full length window on ground level. Ask for a student volunteer to stand outside, close to the window. Trace the volunteer's silhouette on the glass with the grease pencil. Have the student back away from the window about 10 feet and trace again, then another 10 feet and trace yet again. The student's silhouette becomes smaller because of perspective. Usually, perspective is handled through creating foreground (close up), middleground (middle distance), and background (far away). Perspective is also created in more advanced ways by the process of using "vanishing points" or systems measuring how something gets smaller as it moves back in space.

Have students create a series of two drawings using a clear foreground, middleground and background. One drawing will show the perspective accurately portrayed, and one will show the same elements at the same sizes but placed differently on the page, with the perspective skewed. For example, the first drawing might show a person in the foreground, rolling hills and trees in the middleground and mountains in the background. The second drawing would switch the elements around, possibly showing tiny mountains in the foreground and the person in the background (drawn the same size as in the first picture) but placed at the top of the page and now appearing to be a giant. The idea is to demonstrate clearly how perspective works.

Materials
- pencils
- erasers
- grease pencils
- glass door or window

GRID CALVES, KITTENS & KIDS

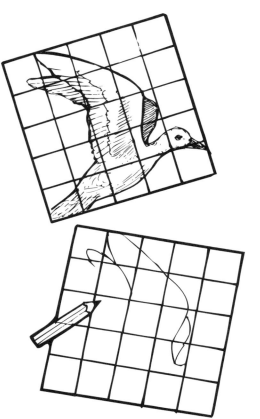

Students may not realize this, but even great "master" artists sometimes have trouble drawing proportions correctly. Using a grid system can help keep proportions accurate and take some of the guess work out of drawing. In this project, students use a grid system to draw an animal of their choice from a photograph.

Artist's studies, with grids drawn across the top of them, still exist. Drawings, such as Jacopo Carucci da Pontormo's *Study for a Female Figure,* show a large grid over the top which was used in the process of transferring the image. Using a grid allowed the artist to keep proportions accurate and to easily enlarge the drawing from the original sketch to a larger wall or canvas without losing its essence. Your artists can use this same effective method to help them draw something new. In this case, the subject is an animal, but this same method may be applied to draw anything.

STUDIO

Ask students to choose a photograph of an animal (*National Geographic* is a good source). It is not a bad idea to start a picture file for this very purpose, so that over time ,you may build up a collection of different images for students. Have each student measure and draw a one-inch (26 millimeters) grid either the size of, or larger than, his or her photograph. The student can use the marker on the acetate overlay. To do this, measure and mark one-inch (26 millimeters) segments from top to bottom and left to right along the edges: then connect the marks. Have students make corresponding grids with pencil on their papers. They should place the acetate grids over the photographs and draw the images by using the grids as guides. This process can be used to draw anything. Save the acetate grids for later re-use.

Materials
- pencils
- erasers
- permanent black markers
- rulers
- 8½" (216 mm) paper
- 8½" (216 mm) clear acetate sheets
- magazine photographs of animals

AESOP'S FABULOUS FABLES

This activity helps your young artists learn to draw animals realistically, yet with emotion. It is not enough to simply copy a photograph of a fox for the project. Students must depict the sly fox who greedily tries to reach for the grapes!

Show students drawings of animals by famous artists and illustrators. Pictures that show animals in an emotional or active way are best. Eugène Delacroix's *Horse Frightened by a Storm*, for example, shows not a prettily posed horse, but an emotionally charged animal. Other suggestions would be animal studies done by Beatrix Potter, or animals drawn for *Fantasia* (the Walt Disney film). The idea is to show realism, but with character and feeling.

STUDIO

Choose a story or stories to read to your class from *Aesop's Fables*. You may hand out copies of the story, but do not include illustrations from the book.

Ask students to portray a scene or scenes from one of the fables and to depict the animals in the story as realistically as possible, while showing the animals' character traits. Your artists must add feeling, life and individuality to the work. This is a challenging exercise, but after completing it your students will be ready to work on the next Disney blockbuster!

Materials
- **pencils**
- **erasers**
- **colored pencils**
- **paper**
- *Aesop's Fables*
- **pictures of animals for reference**

SEASCAPE ESCAPE

Many famous artists have created dramatic and beautiful landscapes where no "land" is present at all—these are "seascapes." For this project, students get to create images of the beautiful blue sea.

Show students some different kinds of drawings of the sea, Winslow Homer's *Perils of the Sea* or *After the Hurricane,* for example. Other artists whose work you might look at are James Abbott McNeill Whistler and Claude Monet. It is interesting to see how different artists portray the sunlight on the rippling waves, boats along the shore, and the life surrounding the sea.

STUDIO

Ask students to create their own seascapes using photographs as guides (unless, of course, it is possible to go to the actual ocean). First, they should lightly sketch their compositions in pencil, and then add the watercolor pencil. A wet brush turns the watercolor pencil into paint and gives a lovely, fluid look when painting the water. Remind students to look carefully at the photographs for details of light, color and texture.

Materials
- pencils
- erasers
- watercolor pencils
- brushes
- heavy paper
- pictures of seashore scenes
- jars of clear water

CARTOONING

CARICATURE BUILDING

Caricatures are fun to create and sure to add humor and hilarity to the classroom. Who has seen a caricature published in a magazine or one drawn at a fair and not laughed? Caricatures are fun, easy-to-create and are based on many of the same principles as realistic portraiture. Even famous artists, such as the Pre-Raphaelites, were known to draw caricatures of one another for fun.

Show the class examples of caricatures—ones that have been drawn at a local fair or amusement park, ones drawn of political figures or celebrities from editorial sections of newspapers and magazines. They will be creating their own caricatures, so ask students what makes a caricature recognizable and what makes the caricature funny. Are there certain traits that are just innately humorous?

STUDIO

Remind the class that in order to create an accurate caricature it is necessary to look very carefully at the subject, just as with a realistic portrait, and they may then choose a feature, or features, to emphasize. If one is drawing a person who seems to have a big nose, then the nose should be drawn so that it is huge! If the person has long hair, make it so long that it stretches to the ground. Have the class select pictures of celebrities and create caricatures—always remind them to look carefully! Lastly, add color with the watercolor pencils or watercolor crayons. Ask the class which caricatures are more successful and why.

Materials
- pencils
- colored pencils or watercolor crayons or pencils
- brushes
- letter-size paper
- pictures of celebrities

GIGGLES WITH SQUIGGLES

In this exercise, students create beautiful, imaginative and funny art out of spontaneous squiggles. They learn to look at all the possibilities that a single line can have.

This project is a good exercise to loosen up students and a great warm-up for "gesture" drawing. Show students examples of art by Henri Matisse, Joan Miró, Paul Klee, and other artists whose works deal with the use of line.

STUDIO

Ask students to make one broad squiggle on the page—one simple line—an abstract gesture. Have them switch drawings with their neighbors. After this has been done, ask students to look at the squiggle closely. What shapes or images do they see? What do the lines suggest to them? Ask them to turn the paper around and examine it from all angles. When they start to see an object, animal, funny face, or design emerge, ask them to turn the squiggle into that thing. Repeat over and over. Students will love to make squiggles into art!

Materials
- pencils
- crayons or markers
- newsprint

CRAZY CARTOON CHARACTERS

What child does not love, or has not, at some point, been fascinated by, cartoon characters? Whether the character is a funny animal like Bugs Bunny, a more realistic-looking action adventure superhero like Superman, or a beautiful princess like Belle from Disney's *Beauty and the Beast*, children can relate to cartoons and to the stories they tell. These characters can portray ideas and stories in ways that are accessible to people of all ages. In this project, students have an opportunity to create their own characters that they can use in their own comic strips or comic books.

Show examples of cartoon characters that have been created throughout the last century. Mickey Mouse, Little Orphan Annie, Buck Rogers, and Dick Tracy are all characters created decades ago and which are still remembered fondly. In some cases, they tell a lot about the times in which they were created. Knowing that Little Orphan Annie was popularized during the Great Depression puts the comic in a new light, as does knowing that Buck Rogers was created before space travel was possible, in a time that looked forward to the day people would land on the moon. Cartoons were used during World War II to teach people slogans, such as "Loose Lips Sink Ships," and to teach safety tips.

STUDIO

When students are ready to begin their own characters, let them brainstorm for a while, sketching and thinking about the kind of characters they want to make. Is the character an animal or human? Or is it some other kind of fantastic creature? Is it silly or more realistic? What qualities does the character have? What is the character's name? After some thought has gone into this, it is good to start by drawing basic shapes and using them as building blocks. Most cartoon characters are based on simple shapes, generally circles and ovals. These basic shapes are then distorted—twisted, stretched and angled to give a character the appearance of motion or direction. Your cartoonists can draw inspiration from their favorite contemporary or classic cartoons. After their characters are designed, the next steps are to "ink" the outlines with marker or some other form of black ink pen and then to fill the inside shapes with colored pencil.

Materials
- **soft pencils**
- **erasers**
- **black ink pens or markers**
- **colored pencils**
- **letter-size sheets of paper**
- **examples of different kinds of cartoon characters**

Comic Strip Cacophony

In the previous project, students worked hard to create their own comic characters. In this project, students use those characters to create their own comic strips or short comic books. They may create cartoons that are humorous or serious.

Refer to books or newspapers with cartoon characters. It is helpful for students to see how other cartoonists space out the progress of their cartoons and how they represent words, ideas and expressions. Your young cartoonists should think about the story they want to portray in the series of drawings. Is it comic or serious? If comic, what is the "punch line" at the end of the story?

STUDIO

Students can begin by drawing the boxes in which their cartoons are framed. Use rulers to measure and draw straight and square boxes (with 90° angles in the corners) that leave enough space for the drawings—longer for more elaborate or more horizontal scenes. Ask students to do a "thumbnail," or small sketch, to plan the layout of their panels before they go on to the final versions. Remember to plan for a white margin on the edges of the paper and between rows of comic strips.

For help re-drawing the characters students created earlier, and to keep the characters consistent, encourage students to remain aware of the proportions of their characters and to keep them constant. Proportion is used in all drawings. It is a way of measuring elements of the drawing. In other words, students should use elements of their characters as a measuring guide. The size of the character's head is one common form of measurement for many different kinds of drawing. The average person is about eight or nine heads tall (the height of the head when added up eight or nine times). Cute, child-like, cartoons often have shorter proportions because children have shorter proportions (Charlie Brown is only about two heads tall). Fashion drawings or bold superheroes can be 12 heads tall or more, lending them a willowy or an imposing look.

Materials
- **soft pencils**
- **erasers**
- **black ink pens or markers**
- **colored pencils**
- **letter-size sheets of paper**
- **rulers**
- **examples of cartoon characters**
- **Crazy Cartoon Characters from page 44**

Optional
- **triangles**
- **T squares**

POKING FUN AT POLITICS

Political cartoons are not only humorous, they make statements or express opinions. In this exercise, students get to make their own political cartoons and express their own opinions through art.

STUDIO

Show students examples of political cartoons from the editorial pages of your local newspaper or from a magazine. Discuss with students what the artists are expressing in their cartoons, and why they choose to show their sentiments through cartoons as opposed to just writing their opinions.

Ask each student to consider an issue—national or local—about which she or he would like to express an opinion and to think of a humorous way of representing it. Your students may wish to depict a situation, public figure or debate in an exaggerated way. It may be helpful to think about the relationships among the characters in the situation and to use a metaphor that shows the artist's opinion. For example, a cartoon representing a student's dislike of cafeteria food might show the students in an emergency room after having eaten lunch. This cartoon clearly shows the artist's opinion.

Materials
- pencils
- erasers
- ink pens
- paper
- editorial pages

SUPERHEROES

Superheroes have long been loved by generations of children and have helped children learn to distinguish between right and wrong. For this project, students design their own superheroes with original talents and traits.

STUDIO

Discuss with students which superheroes they admire and why. What special qualities make a superhero interesting? Ask students to draw their own superheroes with unusual characteristics. They should not be Superman or Wonder Woman clones, but should be original and innovative designs.

Perhaps the superhero looks different than your typical hero; perhaps he or she has unusual talents or uses those talents in a different way. The superhero could be a teacher who uses the power of knowledge and has magical books, or she or he could be an older person or a very young person. A superhero could be in a wheelchair, perhaps a flying wheelchair! Encourage students to be dynamic and innovative in their designs of characters. Urge students to use anatomy reference books to portray musculature in accurate ways, if they want their characters to look realistic.

After your artists have lightly sketched their designs, have them ink in the outlines with black ink pens and fill in the color with markers. They might even wish to add words for their characters.

Materials
- pencils
- markers
- black ink pens
- smooth paper (such as bond paper)
- books on musculature or anatomy

ANIMATE YOUR STUDENTS

As your students progress in their drawing skills from squiggles to the ability to capture gestures, motion and activity, one natural and fun progression is to try an animation project.

STUDIO

Have a student demonstrate an action (taking a step, throwing a ball, etc.) quickly and then in "slow motion." Explain to your students that this is how film, television and cartoon animation work. Animation consists of motions broken down into small pieces which, frame by frame, create a moving picture. This would be a good time for a field trip to an animation studio. If that is not possible, try using a video recorder to slow down the action of a cartoon and view it second by second.

Ask the students to think of a single action to animate in their flip books (small pads of paper). The first "frame" of the animation is the first page of the pad of paper with added drawings on each page, each slightly advancing the gesture until the end of the "flip" finishes the mini-animation. It takes 12 drawings to animate a single second of a cartoon; imagine the thousands of drawings needed to make a feature animated film.

Materials
- **small pads of blank white paper for each student**
- **pencils**
- **pens**
- **markers**

CREATIVE IMAGINATIVE

LEONARDO'S
DAILY LEARNING JOURNAL

Almost all artists use sketchbooks to work out "thumbnail" ideas of compositions, to study something in detail which they will later paint, draw or sculpt more in-depth, or simply to record observations. In this project, students start their own such journals.

Show students pages from Leonardo da Vinci's journal. Da Vinci's journal has been published along with translations. It shows not only his artistic studies but also his ideas for inventions and the notes of his amazing scientific discoveries. The lifelong sketchbook, or learning journal, was for da Vinci something that did not end with one project but that continued to be used as the artist learned and grew.

STUDIO

Ask students to begin collecting drawings in their sketchbooks, studies of things and people they draw from everyday life. They can also record ideas for projects, or scientific observations, like da Vinci did. Have the students keep their sketchbooks for a specific period—a month or so—and check with them individually to see how they are progressing.

Materials
- **pencils or ink pens**
- **erasers**
- **blank journals or notebooks**

ARCHITECTURAL ASPIRATIONS

For this exercise, students draw their own fanciful buildings—houses, mansions or palaces—where they would like to live when they grow up. Practical limitations need not apply—these houses could even exist in outer space!

Show students examples of architectural drawings, Leonardo da Vinci's "Project for a Church" study or Michelangelo's completed "St Peter's" in Rome, for example. Show architecture from as many different styles, places and time periods as possible. Try to look for books which include architects' renderings, books which demonstrate the development of a dream into reality. This may also be a good time for a quick talk about perspective, the idea that objects appear to become smaller as they get farther away from us. Architects draw perspective using many various kinds of systems of measured points and lines that angle back to them. Students need not have extensive knowledge about perspective for this project, but advanced students may wish to investigate this further.

STUDIO

Ask students to design and draw their own fantasy dwellings. They can be as fantastic and imaginative as the students wish. Perhaps a dwelling has amazing space age features, or perhaps it borrows its charms from Renaissance castles. Students must draw neatly, however. Straight lines can be created with rulers and circles drawn with circle templates. This should be done as if it were a plan to be followed by builders. Ask your young architects to make notes on their plans of special features in neat, draftsmanlike lettering. For a special effect, enlarge drawings on a large blue-print copier available at many copy centers.

Materials
- pencils
- erasers
- rulers
- circle templates
- triangles
- smooth paper, such as bond or tracing paper
- books on architecture, which include architects' drawings

Throughout the ages, artists have created many drawings of fabulous mythological beasts, everything from unicorns and mermaids to seamonsters and dragons. For this project, your students use their imaginations to invent their own fantastic creatures.

It is interesting to look at existing drawings of mythological creatures. Every culture seems to have them. Look at some examples with your class, such as Celtic winged lions from illuminated manuscripts, Chinese dragons or the many versions of mermaids painted by John William Waterhouse and other Pre-Raphaelite artists. You may even wish to read stories to your class from mythology about the Minotaur or the Sphinx. While many of these creatures combine attributes of two or more beings, some seem completely invented.

STUDIO

Have your students try to create their own fantastic creatures, getting inspiration from the ones mentioned above. If they are stuck, ask them to think about combining features from several different beings (just as the wings of a bird on a horse creates the mythological Pegasus). Scratchboard is a fun medium for this project because it can add an eerier effect, but this project can be done with any medium—colored pencils work well, too. In fact, you might even want to suggest using colored pencils to add color to the scratched away portions of the compositions.

When students have designed their fantastical creatures, have them come up with names for their creatures and label them.

Materials

- pencils
- pre-prepared scratchboard (or prepare your own by painting the surface of the scratchboard with india ink)
- scratch tool
- books on mythology

Optional
- colored pencils

CREATIVE COSTUMES

Students may not realize this, but every garment they wear, every costume in movies or television, has been drawn by an artist and then created from that design. In this activity, students have an opportunity to create their own fantastic designs for costumes of their choice.

Begin by showing the class books with illustrations of fashion and costume design. It can be interesting to see what was worn decades or centuries ago, and how the concept of what was appealing or attractive has changed. It is funny to think of people shaving their heads to wear powdered wigs, but that was the fashion 200 years ago.

STUDIO

Ask the students to design a costume for a specific purpose, such as a Halloween party or a school play, or for a series of designs that illustrates characters from literature. If the class is reading a play or story that takes place in another time period or culture, all the better because the students can research the time period or country to inspire their work.

Ask your students to draw illustrations of their designs or series of designs and to color them with markers. Each "plate" or page should have only one costume represented.

Materials
- pencils
- erasers
- colored markers
- paper
- books on costumes, fashion, armor, etc.

In this exercise, students get to create their own imaginative drawings on the large open spaces of the schoolyard. Of course, it will wash away with the first rain, leaving only clean pavement and happy memories.

Before you take your class outside to draw, it might be useful to show them the work of "graffiti" artist Keith Haring. Haring created art in the subways of New York City, on sidewalks and on walls. Because his art was technically illegal, he always had to work fast and leave quickly. Luckily, people soon discovered how interesting and meaningful his drawings were and now his work hangs in art museums all over the world. Haring believed that art is for everyone and should be an everyday occurrence for all of us.

STUDIO

Take your students outside and let them draw creatively and imaginatively, as a group or solo. Let them explore, allowing for ideas that come up to be expressed at will. It may also be interesting to discuss with students the trend in contemporary art toward art that exists only temporarily and must be enjoyed in the present—an event—such as the sculptural work of the artist Christo. Enjoy the day, and prepare to be amazed.

Materials
- **sidewalk chalk or chalk pastels**
- **sidewalk or black-top area**

MARVELOUS MACHINE

For this project, students get to design their own ingenious inventions and create technical drawings that describe the inventions' features as well as how they work.

Show students, if you have not already, the journals of Leonardo da Vinci. This artist created many inventions such as flying machines, war machines and even the first helicopter!

STUDIO

Ask your students to create their own inventions—inventions that are as daring as flying to the stars or inventions to simplify cooking breakfast. Each invention must be a clearly labeled and schematically drawn technical drawing. That means that all details and descriptions about its features must be labeled, and it must be measured to be proportionately correct, just as though if it were to be built from these plans.

For an extra exciting touch, take the finished plans to a copy center that makes blueprints and have your own blueprint drawings made of these wonderful machines. The future is being created today with the help of your young inventors!

Materials
- pencils
- erasers
- rulers
- smooth paper, such as bond or tracing paper
- circles, ovals or other templates
- T squares
- triangles

Your students' mission as reporters for the *Time Traveler Times* is to go back in time to report and record with drawings some historical event.

Before the invention of photography and during photography's early stages, artists were relied on to record important events for newspapers. Artists drew pictures of battles like those fought during the Civil War and of events, such as the completion of the railroads that spanned North America. Today, artists still draw in courtrooms and other places where cameras are either not allowed or not well suited.

STUDIO

For this project, each student researches a historical event of her or his choosing and does a series of drawings (at least two) depicting the event, the people involved, and the setting in which it took place. Since these drawings are for a newspaper, they should also have captions.

You may wish to go further with this project and have students write accompanying articles. Bind all of the pages into a finished periodical, or better yet, "publish" it on your school copy machine.

Materials
- **pencils**
- **erasers**
- **black ink pens or markers**
- **books on historical events**

ON COLOR

Color Wheel

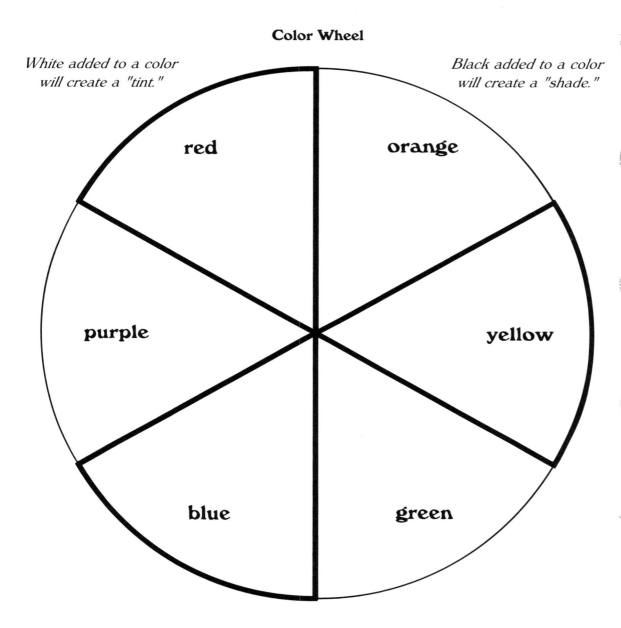

White added to a color will create a "tint."

Black added to a color will create a "shade."

red   orange

purple   yellow

blue   green

The colors, or "hues," labeled within the heavy outlines are called "primary" colors. These colors can be combined to create the other "secondary" colors of the wheel. You can tell which color is "complimentary" to which color by looking to see what is across from it on the wheel. Since red is opposite from green on the wheel, we know that the two are complimentary colors. Mix the two together to make brown, or use them side-by-side for a dazzling effect.

ON COMPOSITION

Static Composition
Note how the objects are centered on the page and there is a lot of blank, empty space.

Dynamic Composition
See how the objects break off of the edges of the page.
They are not centered, but placed in a way
that leads the eye around the image.
All the space is considered—
even the shapes that form the background space.

ON PERSPECTIVE

Objects in the background of this composition are small because things appear to be smaller the farther away they are from the viewer. (Large mountains are depicted as smaller than trees because the mountains are farther away.)

In this simple drawing, one-point perspective is used to show how the rails of the railroad tracks appear to join closer together as they recede.

In order to create more three-dimensional drawings, an artist can incorporate two, three or even more points of perspective.

ON SHADING AND SHADOWS

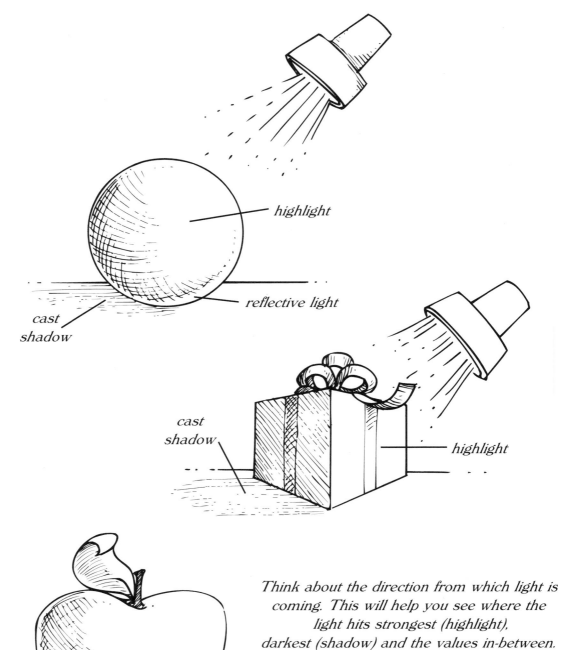

highlight

reflective light

cast shadow

cast shadow

highlight

Think about the direction from which light is coming. This will help you see where the light hits strongest (highlight), darkest (shadow) and the values in-between.

reflective light

cast shadow

highlight

GLOSSARY

abstract: a style of painting, drawing, sculpture, or other art form in which a realistic depiction is not necessary or important; instead, shapes, lines, colors, and textures are formed for their own merit

background: the portion of a drawing that is the farthest away, usually at the top edge of the page

botanical: relating to the world of plants and plant life

calligraphy: a method of producing beautiful and elegant writing by the means of a pen with a chiseled tip—when twisted and twirled this pen creates thicker or thinner lines which add a decorative flourish to the letter forms created

caricature: a funny, exaggerated portrait of someone

commission: to hire an artist to create a piece of artwork, often to commemorate a specific occasion or to create a portrait of a specific person or people

composition: the arrangement of elements in a piece of artwork to form a whole

contour: the edges or outlines of an object, a contour drawing is one which focuses on following the edges of an object.

contrast: the relationship between black and white in an image—"high contrast" refers to sharper blacks and whites and "low contrast" usually means more grays and subtle values.

crosshatching: the creation of short parallel marks placed in opposite directions to create a dark, even, filled pattern

drapery studies: practice drawings created of folded and draped fabric which better enable an artist to render clothing, table cloths or any other such object.

foreground: the portion of a drawing that is the closest to the viewer, usually at the bottom edge of the page

gesture: a simple, quickly drawn mark that indicates a movement or a shape

graffiti art: an art form in which the artist uses public spaces for her or his canvas, such as the subway art created by Keith Haring

impressionism: a school of art founded in late-nineteenth century France by artists who believed in creating art from "impressions" of sunlight reflecting on the world around them. They often used bright colors in large strokes to simulate this glimmering effect.

ink: to trace with ink pen the rough outlines of a pencil-drawn image

middleground: the portion of a drawing that is in the middle distance in relation to the viewer, usually in the middle of the page

negative space: the space that is not the subject of a drawing but that flows around the subject; space not occupied by form

perspective: a system which is used by artists to help simulate the three-dimensional world when working on a two-dimensional surface; a process used to simulate depth and distance.

plate: a term meaning the page or illustration board that an image is drawn on; also refers to engravings which are etched on metal plates

Pre-Raphaelite: a school of art founded in Britain in the late-nineteenth century, centered on creating realistic natural details and subject matter out of romantic stories, legends, and moral truths—the name comes from the desire to go back to a style of art that existed before the time when the artist Raphael lived

proportion: the relation of elements in a drawing to one another, or of elements of the drawing to the subject matter. Proportion can be used to keep things relative and realistic or can be exaggerated for great dramatic effect

resist: a technique in which water-based paint is painted over crayon, oil pastel or other oil-based medium which "resists" the water and so shows through

seascape: a picture in which the ocean, or ocean-related objects are the main subject.

sumi-e: a Japanese word meaning "ink paintings" and referring to a style of painting noted for bold , striking, brushstrokes and uncluttered compositions

texture: a representation of something tactile; portraying the surface qualities of something

thumbnail sketch: a quick, small-sized pencil sketch used to arrange a composition or to help an artist plan out a drawing before he or she begins the final, larger version

tooth: referring to the texture of paper—a paper with a rougher texture as opposed to a smoother one—to which pastels and chalky mediums will better adhere

value: the relative lightness or darkness of a specific color; the porportioned effect of form, light and shade

vanishing points: systems of perspective that use a calculated point, or points, and lines that meet them

zoological: relating to the world of animals

BIBLIOGRAPHY

Ash, Russell. *Toulouse-Lautrec: The Complete Posters*. London: Pavilion Books, 1991.

Brown, Jonathan. Velázquez: *Painter and Courtier*. New Haven, Connecticut: Yale University Press, 1986.

Cawley, John, and Jim Korkis. *How to Create Animation*. Las Vegas, Nevada: Pioneer Books, Inc. 1990.

Durozoi, Gérard. *Toulouse-Lautrec: The Master Works*. Avenel, New Jersey: Crescent Books, 1992.

Eisler, Colin. *The Seeing Hand: A Treasury of Great Master Drawings*. New York: Harper & Row Publishers, 1975.

Hartt, Frederick. *Michelangelo Drawings*. New York: Harry N. Abrams, Inc., 1975.

Jacobus, John. *Matisse*. New York: Harry N. Abrams, Inc., 1983.

Janson, H. W. *History of Art: Survey of the Major Visual Arts from the Dawn of History to the Present Day*. New York: Harry N. Abrams, Inc., 1991.

Julien, Édouard. *Toulouse-Lautrec*. New York: Crown Publishers, Inc., 1991.

Lampugnani, Vittorio Magnago. *Architecture of the 20th Century in Drawings: Utopia and Reality*. New York: Rizzoli International Publications, 1982.

Le Pichon, Yann. *The Real World of the Impressionists: Paintings and Photographs 1848–1918*. New York: Clarkson N. Potter, Inc., 1983.

Lin, Mike W. *Architectural Rendering Techniques: A Color Reference*. New York: Van Nostrand Reinhold, 1985.

Lindemann, Gottfried. *Prints & Drawings: A Pictorial History*. New York: Praeger Publishers, Inc., 1970.

Mannering, Douglas. *The Art of Matisse*. New York: Excalibur Books, 1982.

Mathews, Nancy Mowill. *Mary Cassatt*. New York: Harry N. Abrams, Inc., 1987.

Marks, Claude. *From the Sketchbooks of the Great Artists: A Revealing Collection of Seldom-Seen Sketches by Many of the World's Greatest Artists—from Honnecourt to Cézanne to Nevelson.* New York: Thomas Crowell Company, 1972.

Slive, Seymour. *Drawings of Rembrandt.* New York: Dover Publications, Inc., 1965.

Stuckey, Charles F., and William P. Scott. *Berthe Morisot: Impressionist.* New York: Hudson Hills Press, 1987.

Sutton, Denys. *Edgar Degas: Life and Work.* New York: Rizzoli International Publications, Inc., 1986.

Turner, Nicholas. *Florentine Drawings: of the Sixteenth Century.* New York: Cambridge University Press, 1986.

Watson, Ernest. *Creative Perspective for Artists and Illustrators.* New York: Dover Publications, Inc., 1992.